Quick Smarts

DINOSAURS

Dinosaurs!

Dinosaur means "terrible lizard."
These fantastic animals ruled
the Earth for 160 million years.

Dinosaurs were all reptiles.

They hatched from eggs!

When did dinosaurs live?

The first dinosaurs lived in a time
called the TRIASSIC, a dry period. Then came
the JURASSIC, when the climate was wetter and
milder. There were more forests during this time
and more plants to eat. This led to the arrival of
big, plant-eating dinosaurs (herbivores), and then
the meat eaters (carnivores). Next up was the
CRETACEOUS. This was the time of flowering
plants and of dinos like *T rex* and *Triceratops*.

Dinosaur timeline

Dinosaurs and
mammals evolved

Birds evolved

Triassic period

Jurassic period

245 million years ago

208 million years ago

How big were dinosaurs?

Dinosaurs came in all shapes and sizes. They could be as big as a five-story building, or as small as a chicken. They could walk on two legs or four. They could be quiet plant eaters or the most fearsome hunters.

Where did dinosaurs go?

The dinosaurs died out 65 million years ago! We don't know exactly what caused this. Many scientists think that a giant asteroid hit the Earth, causing the climate to change.

Old fossil!

We understand dinosaurs from their fossils. Fossils are the remains of dead animals from millions of years ago, turned into stone.

Dinosaurs may live on today in the form of birds—there could be a descendant of *T rex* in a tree or in your backyard!

Dinosaurs became extinct

People evolved

Cretaceous period

Now

145 million years ago

65 million years ago

T rex

Tyrannosaurus rex means "tyrant lizard king." No wonder— at 40 ft (12 m) long, it was one of the largest meat-eating dinosaurs that ever lived.

T rex's **mouth** was so **big** that a whole COW could fit inside.

Say "aaarghh"!

T rex's mouth contained 50 teeth—some were the size of a banana! Its teeth were four times as big as a tiger's. (You wouldn't want to be its dentist!)

4

and its

Its head was up to **5 ft (1.5 m)** long . . .

. tongue

jaws were up to 4 ft **(1.2 m)** long .

. . . . . jaw

Bite marks on fossils suggest that *T rex* could **bite** through **solid bone!**

Meat and no veg

T rex ate a diet of meat, meat, and more meat. It feasted on other large dinosaurs including *Triceratops*. A hungry *T rex* could chomp its way through the

A *T rex*

That's as

The **frill** protecting its neck was made of bone covered with skin.

frill

When attacked, *Triceratops* would lower its head. Even *T rex* would find it hard to get past those horns!

11

Cheeky!

Triceratops pulled up tough plants using its beak, and sliced them into pieces with its powerful jaws. Although it had no front teeth, its cheeks were packed with between 400 and 800 teeth arranged in rows, which slid past each other like scissor blades.

Triceratops

Lots of

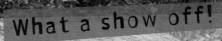

What a show off!

Triceratops may have used its frill to protect it from attackers, or even to show off and impress other dinosaurs!

Did you know?

Fossilized *T rex* poop contained chunks of bones, which may have come from the neck frill of a *Triceratops*! The *T rex* had either killed the *Triceratops* or snacked on one that had already died.

probably roamed together in **herds.**

remains have been found, but no

fully complete **skeletons.**

Ready to fight!

Triceratops comes from a family of dinosaurs called "ceratopians"—meaning "horned face." *Triceratops* was a plant eater, but that didn't mean that it was peace-loving—lots of *Triceratops* skulls and neck frills have been found with damage and scars, showing that they fought each other over territory and mates. *Triceratops* had horns like a rhino and weighed about the same as an elephant—what a combination!

Elephant

Rhinoceros

Lots of dinosaurs were vegetarians but they didn't eat grass as it hadn't evolved yet.

14

Its body was solid muscle but its bones were hollow, just like a chicken's.

Thick skin

T rex had skin that was rough and bumpy like an alligator's, making it very hard to bite through. And you'd have to be really stupid to try to bite a *T rex*!

weighed about 15,400 lb (7,000 kg).

heavy as the heaviest land animal

on Earth today . . . an elephant.

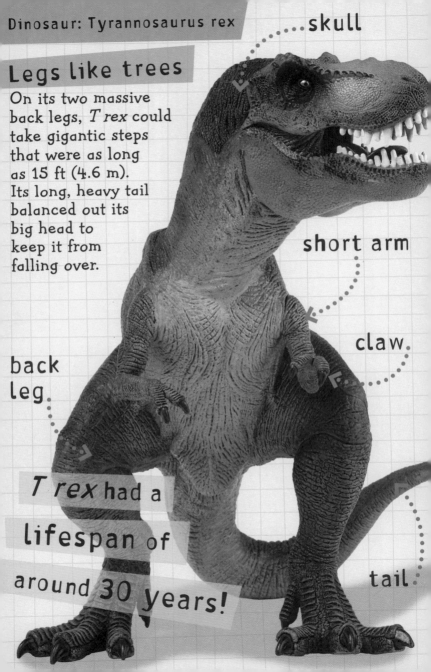

skull

Legs like trees

On its two massive back legs, *T rex* could take gigantic steps that were as long as 15 ft (4.6 m). Its long, heavy tail balanced out its big head to keep it from falling over.

short arm

claw

back leg

T rex had a lifespan of around 30 years!

tail

Quick Smarts

Pronunciation: Tie-RAN-owe-SORE-uss REX

Type: A meat-eating predator (an animal that kills other animals for food).

Existed: About 68–65 million years ago (Late Cretaceous period).

Size: Up to 40 ft (12 m) long and about 18³/₈ ft (5.6 m) tall. That's about seven times longer than the average man. They could weigh 15,400 lb (7,000 kg).

Fossils: Found in the USA and Canada. Only 20 near complete *T rex* specimens have been found.

Diet: Carnivore (meat eater). Ate other large dinosaurs, like *Triceratops*.

Weapons: Huge size and strength; massive mouth with 50 solid teeth; and jaws that were twice as powerful as those of a great white shark.

Q: What do you get when dinosaurs crash cars?

A: Tyrannosaurus wreck!

9

Triceratops

With its sharp horns, huge head plate, and massive body, *Triceratops* (meaning "three-horned face") must have been a scary sight—even for other dinosaurs!

horn

Triceratops had **horns** that were as **long** as **hockey** sticks.

Turtle-y awesome!

Triceratops was the size of an elephant, but its mouth looked like a turtle's beak. This was because it had no front teeth.

10

beak

Quick Smarts

Pronunciation: Try-SERRA-tops

Type: A horned, plant-eating dinosaur.

Existed: About 65 million years ago (Late Cretaceous period).

Size: A fully grown *Triceratops* was about 30 ft (9 m) long and weighed 12,125 lb (5,500 kg)—that's as heavy as an African elephant. Its massive skull could be over 10 ft (3 m) long.

Fossils: All found in western North America.

Diet: Herbivore (plant eater). Ate plants such as palms and ferns.

Weapons: Huge and powerful body; three long, sharp horns; and a neck frill with diamond-shaped, bony spikes.

Q: What do you get if you cross a *Triceratops* with a kangaroo?

A: A Tricera-hops!

Spinosaurus

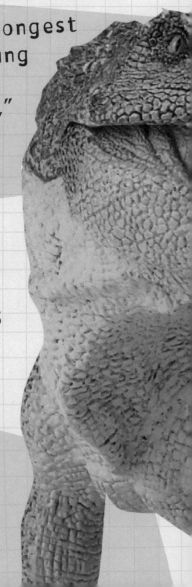

Spinosaurus is the longest of all the meat-eating dinosaurs. Its name means "spiny lizard," and is taken from the large spines along its back.

The spines could have been as long as 6 ft (1.8 m).

Big head!

Spinosaurus had one of the longest heads of any carnivorous (meat-eating) dinosaur—it was 5¾ ft (1.75 m) long! That's the average height of an adult woman!

16

spine

Spinosaurus
T rex
Triceratops
Stegosaurus
Velociraptor

The big one!

Spinosaurus was much longer than *T rex*—around 59 ft (18 m) in length. (But they could never have met, because *T rex* lived 35 million years later.)

Spinosaurus had cone-shaped teeth that were better at stabbing than cutting.

Sail or hump?

The spines probably had skin covering them like a sail. But some scientists think that they may have been covered in muscle and formed a hump—like the hump on a water buffalo.

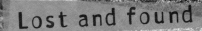

Lost and found

Spinosaurus bones were first found in 1912, but all the remains were destroyed in World War Two. Some bones have been found since, but mostly from the skull.

Spinosaurus may have turned its spines towards the sun to help it warm up!

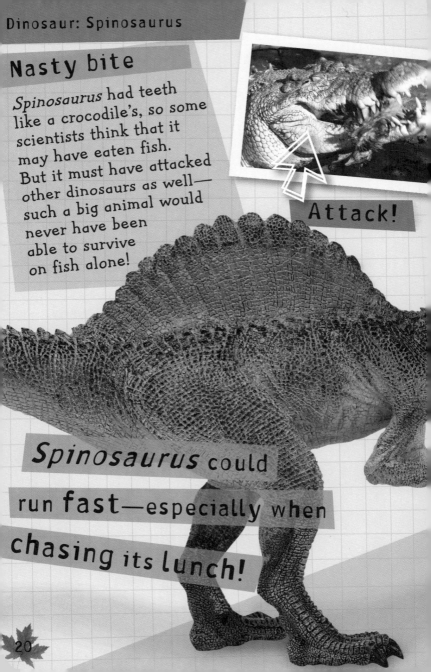

Nasty bite

Spinosaurus had teeth like a crocodile's, so some scientists think that it may have eaten fish. But it must have attacked other dinosaurs as well—such a big animal would never have been able to survive on fish alone!

Attack!

Spinosaurus could run **fast**—especially when chasing its lunch!

20

Quick Smarts

Pronunciation: SPY-no-SORE-uss

Type: A large, meat-eating predator.

Existed: About 100 million years ago (Middle Cretaceous period).

Size: Up to 59 ft (18 m) long—that's about 30 adult paces long. With its sail, it stood 20 ft (6 m) high, and it weighed about 8,800 lb (4,000 kg).

Fossils: Found in North Africa. The first fossil was found in Egypt and other bones have been found in Morocco.

Diet: Carnivore (meat eater). Ate dinosaurs and large fish.

Weapons: Fearsome size (it was the longest meat-eating dinosaur ever); huge, crocodile-like teeth; and powerful jaws. Just very, very scary.

Q: What do you call a *Spinosaurus* with headphones on?

A: Anything you want. It can't hear you.

21

Brachiosaurus

Brachiosaurus was one of the largest, heaviest land animals ever. Its name means "arm lizard," because its front legs are longer than its back legs.

Its **neck** was made of **hollow**

··· long neck

Gentle giant

With its neck stretched forwards, *Brachiosaurus* could be 82 ft (25 m) long. When it reached up high, it could be 42⅝ ft (13 m) high—about the height of three double-decker buses on top of one another.

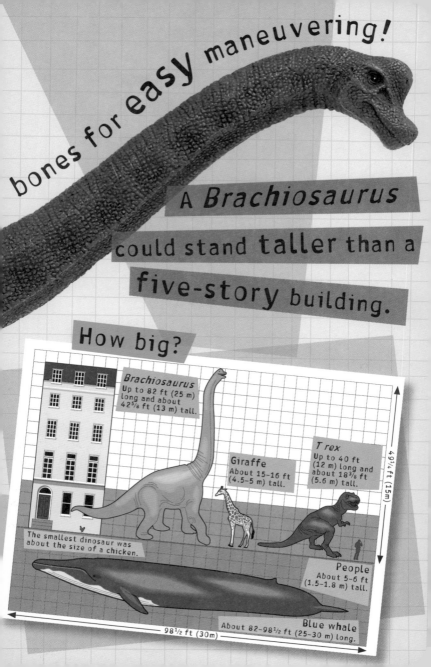

bones for easy maneuvering!

A *Brachiosaurus* could stand **taller** than a **five-story** building.

How big?

Brachiosaurus
Up to 82 ft (25 m) long and about 42⅝ ft (13 m) tall.

Giraffe
About 15–16 ft (4.5–5 m) tall.

T rex
Up to 40 ft (12 m) long and about 18⅜ ft (5.6 m) tall.

The smallest dinosaur was about the size of a chicken.

People
About 5–6 ft (1.5–1.8 m) tall.

49¼ ft (15 m)

98½ ft (30 m)

About 82–98½ ft (25–30 m) long.

Blue whale

A **fully** grown *Brachiosaurus* **weighed** up to 82,000 lb (37,200 kg)— that's the **same** as 6 African **elephants!**

Think big!

The *Brachiosaurus* in the Humboldt Museum, Germany, is the tallest mounted skeleton in the world. It was found in Tanzania, Africa.

Sauropods

Brachiosaurus was a sauropod—
a huge, four-legged, plant-eating
dinosaur. Other well-known sauropods
include *Diplodocus* and *Apatosaurus*.
Sauropod fossils have been found on
every continent except Antarctica.

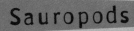

Brachiosaurus could use its
huge tail like a whip
to strike **predators.**

Who nose?

Just like us, *Brachiosaurus* had nostrils.
But unlike us, its nostrils were above
its eyes! (Imagine having a nose on
your forehead!) Some scientists once
thought this helped in the water—
acting like a kind of snorkel. But others
think that *Brachiosaurus* lived on land,
because in water, its legs would have
stuck in the sand or mud!

Giraffe

You want more?

Brachiosaurus was thought to be the biggest dinosaur ever. However, scientists have found four neck bones from an even bigger animal called *Sauroposeidon*. It could stand 60 ft (18 m) tall—18 ft (5 m) taller than *Brachiosaurus*. The bones were so big that scientists first thought they were fossilized tree trunks!

Like a giraffe ... only bigger

With its long front legs, *Brachiosaurus* stood like a giraffe—only three times taller!

Brachiosaurus used its **chisel**-like teeth to eat the tops of fir, pine, and redwood trees.

long
front
leg

Quick Smarts

Pronunciation: BRACH-ee-owe-SORE-uss

Type: A huge, plant-eating sauropod.

Existed: About 150 million years ago (Late Jurassic period).

Size: Up to 82 ft (25 m) long and about $42\frac{5}{8}$ ft (13 m) tall. It could weigh between 70,000–82,000 lb (31,750–37,200 kg).

Fossils: Found throughout the world, especially North America and Africa.

Diet: Herbivore (plant eater). Ate treetop plants.

Weapons: It was big, very big, huge, and massive. (Have we mentioned that it was big?) The point is that it didn't need weapons—although its huge tail could have been used like a whip.

Q: What should you do if you find a dinosaur in your bed?

A: Find somewhere else to sleep!

Stegosaurus

The name *Stegosaurus* means "roof reptile." It was given this name because scientists first thought that the long, bony plates lay flat on its back, like the tiles on a roof.

Stegosaurus was the size

beak-like mouth

small head and tiny brain

A bit thick

Relative to the size of its body, *Stegosaurus* had the smallest brain of any dinosaur. Its body was as big as a bus, but its brain was the size of a walnut!

of a double-decker **bus!**

plate

Did you know?

A *Stegosaurus* tail was armed with large spikes, which it used to smash into enemies in self-defense.

Well protected

As well as plates and spikes, *Stegosaurus* had bony studs around its throat. These studs helped to protect it from the attacking teeth and claws of meat-eating dinosaurs like *Allosaurus*!

Stegosaurus

Blood may

Mysterious plates

Stegosaurus had bony back plates, which contained many little, tube-like tunnels. Did they act as a cooling system? Did they change color to attract another *Stegosaurus*? Were they some kind of armor? No one knows for sure!

...plates were filled with tubes.

...have pumped through these to

...cool it down—like a car radiator.

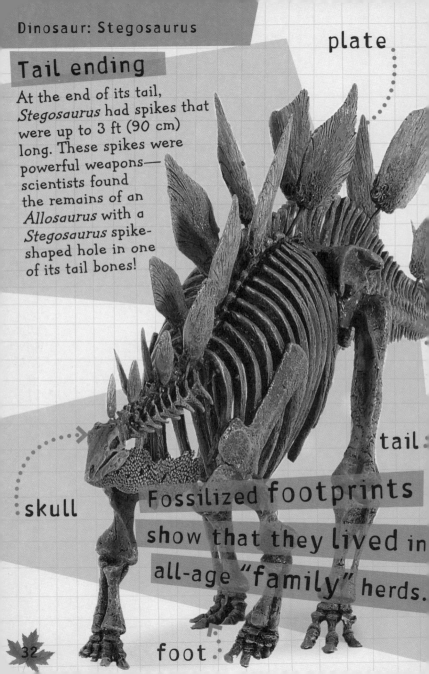

plate

Tail ending

At the end of its tail, *Stegosaurus* had spikes that were up to 3 ft (90 cm) long. These spikes were powerful weapons—scientists found the remains of an *Allosaurus* with a *Stegosaurus* spike-shaped hole in one of its tail bones!

skull

tail

Fossilized footprints show that they lived in all-age "family" herds.

foot

32

Quick Smarts

Pronunciation: STEG-owe-SORE-uss

Type: A large, armored, plant-eating dinosaur.

Existed: About 150 million years ago (Late Jurassic period).

Size: About 14 ft (4 m) tall, with spikes on its tail that were as long as 3 ft (90 cm)—that's about as long as you! It weighed about 10,000 lb (4,500 kg).

Fossils: Found in North America, mainly in Colorado, Utah, and Wyoming.

Diet: Herbivore (plant eater). Ate mosses, ferns, conifers, and cycads (flowerless plants).

Weapons: It was big, and its spine plates would have made it look even bigger. If that didn't scare the attackers off, there was always that vicious, spiked tail . . .

Q: Which dinosaur can't stay out in the rain?

A: Stegosaur-rust!

Velociraptor

Velociraptor means "speedy thief." They hunted in packs, working together to bring down larger prey.

It was one of the **smartest dinosaurs** because of the **size of** its **brain.**

long teeth

Small, but deadly

Velociraptor were only about 3¼ ft (1 m) tall, or the size of a large dog. But they were fierce enough to kill much bigger dinosaurs!

34

It was one of the **fastest** dinosaurs.

Did **you** know?

Velociraptor were featured in the film *Jurassic Park*. The filmmakers made them look four times bigger so they'd be more scary.

We're hooked!

Velociraptor belonged to a group of dinosaurs known as the "maniraptoran"—meaning "grasping hand." But I wouldn't shake its hand if I were you. Its most frightening weapon was a 3½ in (9 cm) long hook-like, ultrasharp claw on each foot!

Over **short** distances, *Velociraptor* could run as fast as an **Olympic** sprinter.

Frighteningly fast

Velociraptor had hollow bones, like birds. That meant they were very light and could move fast. Running on their two back legs, they may have been able to reach speeds of 40 mph (60 kph).

Velociraptor is known to have preyed on plant eaters.

Birdlike nests

Like birds, *Velociraptor* tended nests of eggs. But you wouldn't want to go bird-watching near these guys—they could tear you into pieces!

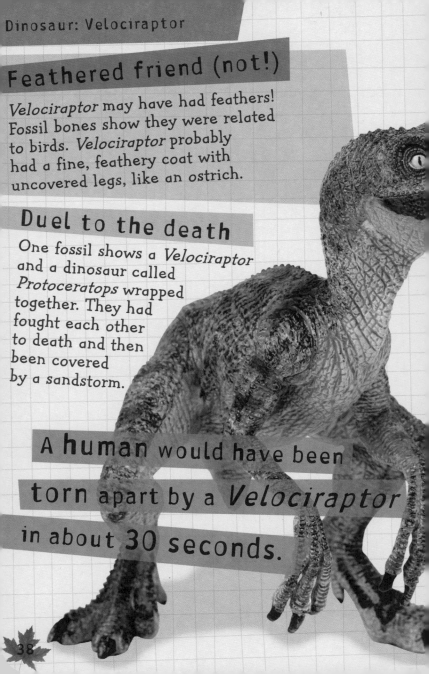

Feathered friend (not!)

Velociraptor may have had feathers! Fossil bones show they were related to birds. *Velociraptor* probably had a fine, feathery coat with uncovered legs, like an ostrich.

Duel to the death

One fossil shows a *Velociraptor* and a dinosaur called *Protoceratops* wrapped together. They had fought each other to death and then been covered by a sandstorm.

A **human** would have been torn apart by a *Velociraptor* in about **30 seconds.**

Quick Smarts

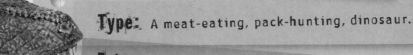

Pronunciation: Vel-0-si-RAP-tor

Type: A meat-eating, pack-hunting, dinosaur.

Existed: About 85–80 million years ago (Middle Cretaceous period).

Size: Up to 6 ft (1.8 m) long and about 3¼ ft (1 m) tall—about the size of a large dog, like a Great Dane. It weighed 15.4–33 lb (7–15 kg).

Fossils: Found in Mongolia, Russia, and China.

Diet: Carnivore (meat eater). Ate herbivores such as *Protoceratops*.

Weapons: Razor-sharp teeth; long, hooked toe; powerful hands with sharp claws to slash, pierce, and tear; and the ability to hunt in organized packs at high speed.

Q: Where did the *Velociraptor* buy things?

A: At a dino-store!

39

Parasaurolophus

Parasaurolophus was a weird looking dinosaur. It had a duck-like mouth and an extremely long, hollow, bony crest. It may also have had webbed feet!

nostrils

The crest may have acted like a trumpet, used to warn others of danger, a bit like honking a car horn!

Nosy!

Parasaurolophus had really long nostrils! Tubes from the nostril opening went to the top of the crest and back down. These hollow tubes were probably used to communicate with the rest of the herd!

40

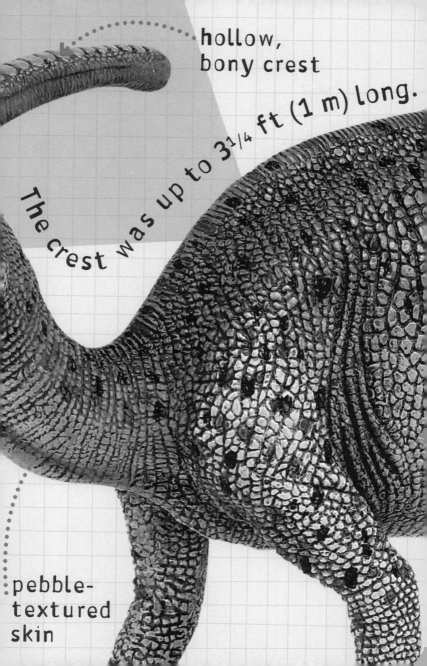

hollow, bony crest

The crest was up to 3¼ ft (1 m) long.

pebble-textured skin

Parasaurolophus lived

A leafy lunch

Parasaurolophus was a herbivore. Fossilized remains show that the contents of its stomach consisted mainly of plants. It ate pine needles, leaves, and twigs.

Parasaurolophus had no natural defenses. It relied on its sight and hearing.

All together now

Parasaurolophus probably gathered together in large herds. Imagine the noise made by an entire orchestra of these dinos—all honking through their built-in trumpets!

Chew on this!

At the front of its mouth, *Parasaurolophus* had a hard beak. Further back were hundreds of teeth in up to 40 rows. These were used to chew up all those tough plants.

Mighty crest

The crest on a *Parasaurolophus* head was up to 3¼ ft (1 m) long. That's probably as long as YOU are! Some experts think females had smaller crests than males.

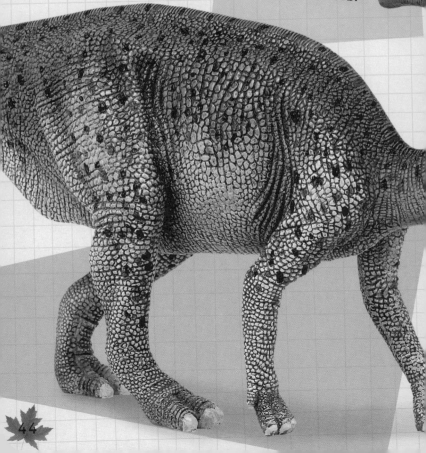

44

Quick Smarts

Pronunciation: Par-a-SORE-owe-LOAF-uss

Type: A plant-eating, herd-dwelling dinosaur.

Existed: About 75 million years ago (Late Cretaceous period).

Size: About 36 ft (11 m) long and 17 ft (5.2 m) tall. It weighed about 7,700 lb (3,500 kg).

Fossils: Found in North America, especially Alberta in Canada, also New Mexico and Utah in the United States.

Diet: Herbivore (plant eater). Ate leaves, twigs, and ferns.

Weapons: None really! Probably a good sense of smell and that honking horn to warn others of danger.

Q: What makes more noise than a *Parasaurolophus*?

A: TWO *Parasaurolophus*!

Ankylosaurus

Ankylosaurus was as big as a tank, and with its heavily armored skin, it was built like a tank as well.

Its powerful tail could probably

armored spike

46

Let's go clubbing!

Ankylosaurus had a tail that ended in a huge ball of bone about 1⅝ ft (50 cm) long, wrapped in tough skin. It was used as a wrecking ball to demolish its opponents!

break the leg of a *T rex.*

clubbed tail

Coat of armor

Its plated armor protected *Ankylosaurus* from the bites and kicks of an attacking dinosaur, and its head was like a box of heavily armored bone. Even a *T rex* would have lost some teeth breaking through *Ankylosaurus* armor.

Soft belly

Only its underbelly was unplated. Flipping it over was the only way to wound *Ankylosaurus*.

47

With its **spiky** back and **tough** skin, Ankylosaurus was the **best-defended** dino!

short neck

toothless, beaked mouth

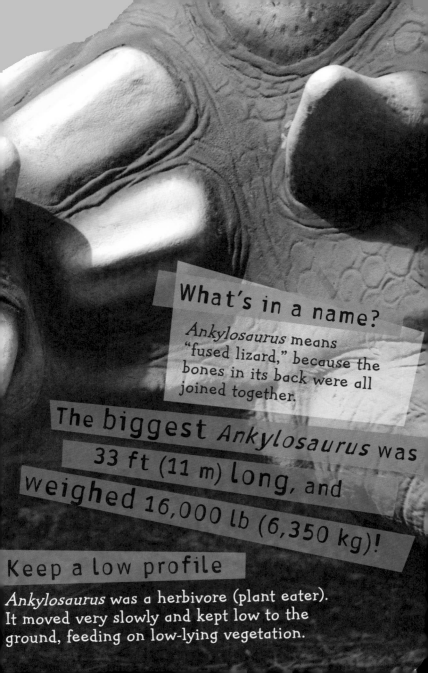

What's in a name?

Ankylosaurus means "fused lizard," because the bones in its back were all joined together.

The biggest *Ankylosaurus* was 33 ft (11 m) long, and weighed 16,000 lb (6,350 kg)!

Keep a low profile

Ankylosaurus was a herbivore (plant eater). It moved very slowly and kept low to the ground, feeding on low-lying vegetation.

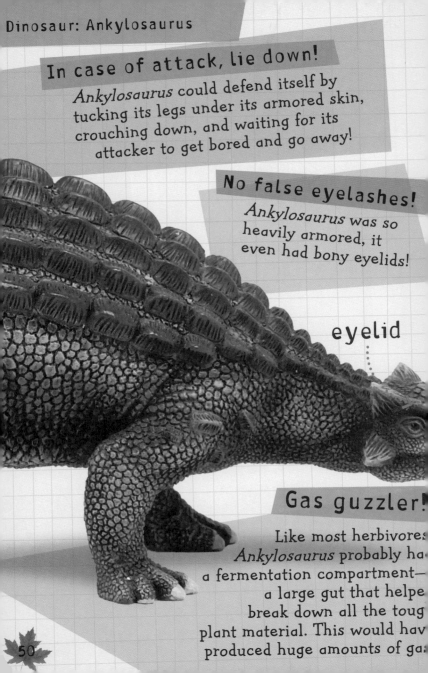

In case of attack, lie down!

Ankylosaurus could defend itself by tucking its legs under its armored skin, crouching down, and waiting for its attacker to get bored and go away!

No false eyelashes!

Ankylosaurus was so heavily armored, it even had bony eyelids!

eyelid

Gas guzzler!

Like most herbivores, *Ankylosaurus* probably ha a fermentation compartment— a large gut that helpe break down all the toug plant material. This would hav produced huge amounts of gas

Quick Smarts

Pronunciation: An-KIE-loh-SORE-uss

Type: A plant-eating, armored dinosaur.

Existed: About 100 million years ago (Middle Cretaceous period).

Size: Around 23 ft (7 m) long, with a weight of over 13,200 lb (6,000 kg)—that's heavier than an elephant. Imagine an armadillo that size!

Fossils: Found in western North America.

Diet: Herbivore (plant eater). Ate low-lying vegetation.

Weapons: Heavily armored skin; wrecking ball club at the end of the tail; and two small horns on the head.

Q: What did the *Ankylosaurus* say after falling over?

A: "I'm dino-sore!"

Allosaurus

Allosaurus was one of the largest, scariest killers ever! It was a carnivore, which means it ate meat—and lots of it!

Allosaurus could open its mouth wide enough to swallow a wild pig in one gulp!

A right mouthful!

Allosaurus had about 40 teeth, all of which had sharp edges, like a saw. Its teeth often fell out during attacks—luckily it could just grow new ones!

horn⋯⋯⋯⋯

sawlike
teeth

Did you know?

In 1991, scientists discovered an almost complete *Allosaurus* skeleton, which they called "Big Al." Big Al had been in lots of fights—he had broken ribs and injuries to his feet, claws, and hip.

Good hunting!

Allosaurus probably hunted in packs! Their short, powerful arms ended in three-fingered, hook-like claws, which they used to hold down their prey while their teeth started chomping!

Fossilized bones have been found with *Allosaurus* bite marks in them!

A pair of shades

Sticking out from its head and hanging just over the eyes were a pair of horns. Scientists think these may have acted as sunshades. Or it may be that the horns were different colors, depending on whether the *Allosaurus* was a boy or a girl!

Beastly feet

Allosaurus was a "theropod" ("beast-feet") dinosaur. These dinosaurs walked on two legs and had small, powerful arms with sharp claws.

Not your average dino

Allosaurus means "different lizard." That's because the bones in its back were different from other dinosaurs.

skull

short arm

Allosaurus was a brainbox among dinosaurs!

three-fingered hand

56

Quick Smarts

Pronunciation: Al-owe-SORE-uss

Type: A fierce, meat-eating predator.

Existed: About 140 million years ago (Late Jurassic period).

Size: Around 40 ft (12 m) long and 16³⁄₈ ft (5 m) tall. That's about the size of a double-decker bus!

Fossils: Found in North America.

Diet: Carnivore (meat eater). Ate large herbivore dinosaurs.

Weapons: Huge size; massive mouth with 40 razor-sharp teeth; and powerful forearms ending in three 15 cm (6 in) long claws.

Q: Which dinosaur slept all day?

A: The dino-snore!

Deinonychus

Deinonychus means "terrible claw." It's named for the huge curved claw on both its feet.

Deinonychus had 60 curved, knifelike teeth that it used to slice its food.

Bird-brain

Deinonychus was covered in feathers, like a bird. It stood about 5 ft (1.5 m) high and could move really fast.

curved teeth

Deinonychus was built to kill!

jaw

Did you know?
Deinonychus grew to about 10–15 ft (3–4 m) in length, but it only weighed about 165 lb (75 kg), which is just a bit more than a human.

Deinonychus hunted large, plant-eating dinosaurs.

Terrible teamwork!

At one fossil site, scientists found the remains of a *Tenontosaurus* (a large herbivore dinosaur) and four *Deinonychus* teeth. Scientists think that a pack of *Deinonychus* attacked and killed this *Tenontosaurus*.

Deinonychus would take down their prey in packs by leaping on their victim's back!

Evil claw!

The large hooked claw on the second toe of a *Deinonychus* foot could be held upright when it was running, then lowered to stab and kill its prey.

Toe-curling

Deinonychus walked on two thin, birdlike legs. When running, it turned up its huge claw and ran on the other toes.

Top tail!

Deinonychus had a long, narrow tail that it held straight out behind its body. Its tail kept it balanced, helping it to turn incredibly quickly.

feathers

Brainiac

Deinonychus had a large brain for a dinosaur. This means it could have learned how to do things better—like hunt!

Deinonychus was almost certainly feathered!

claw

Quick Smarts

Pronunciation: Die-NON-i-kuss

Type: A small, meat-eating hunter.

Existed: About 100–120 million years ago (Early Cretaceous period).

Size: About 5 ft (1.5 m) high, but 10–15 ft (3–4 m) in length—that's as long as a hatchback car. It weighed about 165 lb (75 kg), or about the same as an adult.

Fossils: Found in western United States.

Diet: Carnivore (meat eater). Ate other herbivore dinosaurs.

Weapons: Fast runner; hunted in packs; and had a huge claw on each foot, which was probably used to help finish off its victims after a long chase.

Q: What is the best way to talk to a *Deinonychus*?

A: From a very, very long way away!

Index

Quick Smarts

ULTIMATE

CHALLENGE

DINOSAURS

Quick smarts for your brainy parts

Quick Smarts

DINOSAURS

Stretch your smarts to

snapping point with the

Quick Smarts Dino Challenge!

☺ ☺

When you see this symbol, it's a good idea to tackle the challenge with a friend or in teams, with one person acting as quizmaster. You'll find all the answers in the back of the book.

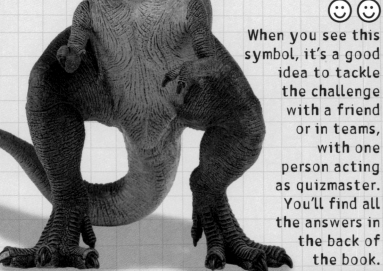

Quick smarts for your brainy parts

Brainy or Bogus

Some of these dino facts are true (as far as we know), and some we've just made up. Can you sort the facts from the fakes?

Check the box—then check your answers.

	Brainy	Bogus
1. The tiniest dinosaurs were as small as chickens.	☐	☐
2. Dinosaurs hatched from eggs.	☐	☐
3. *Velociraptor* had a fur pouch on its back for storing snacks.	☐	☐
4. *T rex* used its tail to floss its teeth.	☐	☐
5. *Parasaurolophus* had up to 40 rows of teeth.	☐	☐
6. *Deinonychus*'s favorite meal was other dinosaurs.	☐	☐
7. *Ankylosaurus* attacked its enemies using a huge ball at the end of its tail.	☐	☐

8. *Spinosaurus* had teeth like a crocodile.

   Brainy ☐ Bogus ☐

9. Dinosaurs only pooped at night.

   Brainy ☐ Bogus ☐

10. *Triceratops* had no front teeth.

   Brainy ☐ Bogus ☐

11. *Brachiosaurus* had a fear of spiders.

   Brainy ☐ Bogus ☐

12. *Velociraptor* was as heavy as an elephant.

   Brainy ☐ Bogus ☐

13. An *Allosaurus* head had built-in sunshades.

   Brainy ☐ Bogus ☐

14. King Henry the 8th of England kept the last *Velociraptor* in the grounds of Buckingham Palace in London.

   Brainy ☐ Bogus ☐

3

Splat Attack

Eeeew! Looks like these dinosaurs have taken a mud bath! See if you can find *T rex, Stegosaurus, Brachiosaurus, Allosaurus,* and *Triceratops* under the slimy splats!

1.

2.

4

3.

4.

5.

5

Brain-Buster 😊😊

Earn over 2,000 points in this ultimate Smart Challenge!

Answer the questions below, and add up your scores as you go along. The last question is worth 1,000 points. But beware! If you get a question wrong, you're out of the quiz and will lose everything!

For **50** points . . .

Scientists have learned about dinosaurs through the discovery of . . .

A. drawings in caves.
B. fossils.
C. photos.
D. pre-historic video footage.

Score [　　　]

For **100** points . . .

Dinosaur means . . .

A. "big mouth."
B. "terrible lizard."
C. "big, itchy scab."
D. "ancient monster."

Score [　　　]

For **200** points . . .

How many years ago did the dinosaurs die out?

A. 65
B. 650
C. 6,500
D. 65,000,000

Score [　　　]

6

For **300** points . . .

What was the most unusual feature of a *Triceratops* face?

A. It was very spotted.
B. It was very pink.
C. It was shaped like a doughnut.
D. It had three horns.

Score ☐

For **500** points . . .

What was the most likely purpose of the hollow, bony crest belonging to *Parasaurolophus*?

A. To suck up drinks, like a big straw.
B. To hide its food.
C. To honk like a car horn.
D. To store boogers.

Score ☐

For **1,000** points . . .

Ankylosaurus had skin that was . . .

A. like a soft blanket.
B. bumpy and blotchy.
C. like armor.
D. sticky and slimy.

Score ☐

Total score ▶ ☐

7

Clued Up! ☺ ☺

Can you identify the following dinos?

You can use a maximum of five clues to guess the answer. Get the answer right after the first clue, and you'll score five points. Take five clues, and you'll score just one!

Dinosaur 1

Clues

Points

1. I lived in the Late Jurassic period, around 150 million years ago.

☐ (5pts)

2. My name means "roof reptile."

☐ (4pts)

3. I have bony studs around my throat.

☐ (3pts)

4. I have large, dangerous spikes at the end of my tail.

☐ (2pts)

5. My body is as big as a bus, but my brain is the size of a walnut.

☐ (1pt)

Clues   Dinosaur 2

Points

1. I am a meat eater and can weigh 15,400 lb (7,000 kg).   ☐ (5pts)

2. I have hollow bones like a chicken.   ☐ (4pts)

3. I am 40 ft (12 m) long and have bumpy skin, like an alligator.   ☐ (3pts)

4. My name means "tyrant lizard king."   ☐ (2pts)

5. I have two massive back legs and two very short arms.   ☐ (1pt)

Clues   Dinosaur 3

Points

1. I am a plant eater.   ☐ (5pts)

2. I have up to 800 teeth.   ☐ (4pts)

3. I have a big frill around my head.   ☐ (3pts)

4. I lived about 65 million years ago in North America.   ☐ (2pts)

5. My name means "three-horned face."   ☐ (1pt)

9

Dinosaur 4

Clues

Points

1. My nose is above my eyes. (5pts)

2. I am taller than a five-story building. (4pts)

3. Fully grown, I can weigh as much as six elephants. (3pts)

4. I am one of the biggest dinosaurs ever, but I only eat plants. (2pts)

5. I have a long neck. (1pt)

Dinosaur 5

Clues

Points

1. I am one of the smartest dinosaurs. (5pts)

2. I am small, but I move fast. (4pts)

3. My name means "speedy thief." (3pts)

4. I am a carnivore, and I hunt in vicious packs. (2pts)

5. I look like an enormous bird. (1pt)

10

Clues — Dinosaur 6

Points

1. I am as big as a tank. (5pts)

2. I am a plant eater. (4pts)

3. I have a massive ball of bone at the end of my tail. (3pts)

4. My underbelly is soft, but the rest of me is covered in armored spikes. (2pts)

5. I have bony eyelids. (1pt)

Clues — Dinosaur 7

Points

1. I have one of the longest heads of all dinosaurs. (5pts)

2. I've got huge teeth like a crocodile. (4pts)

3. My name means "spiny lizard." (3pts)

4. I am the longest of all the meat-eating dinosaurs. (2pts)

5. I have huge spines along my back. (1pt)

11

Laughosaurus

What did dinosaurs use to cut down trees?

Dino-saws!

Why did the *T rex* smell so bad?

Because it was ex-stinked.

What do you call a fossil that watches TV all day?

Lazy bones!

Why are museums full of old dinosaur bones?

Because the new ones are too expensive!

What do you call a dinosaur in tight shoes?

A Myfeetaresaurus!

How did the *Allosaurus* like his steaks?

Roarrrrr!

Dino Dinners

Look at the list below. Pick six things you think a *T rex* would eat for its dinner. Then fit the words into the grid, going left to right. Choose the correct meals and the yellow box will spell a word describing how you'd feel if you met a Rex with the rumbles!

Apples	Potatoes	Ham
Eggs	Carrots	Duck
Toast	Sausage	Cabbage
Biscuits	Chicken	Rabbit

	a				g			
	h		c					
				m				
							i	
					g			
						k		

Answer here!

13

Multi-Choice Challenge 😊😊

Bend your brain with this fiendish multiple-choice quiz!

1. *Spinosaurus* had large spines . . .

a. along its nose.
b. along its back.
c. along its ears.

2. *Deinonychus* means . . .

a. "terrible claw."
b. "terrible breath."
c. "terribly hungry."

3. An *Allosaurus* mouth was wide enough to swallow . . .

a. a car.
b. a pig.
c. another *Allosaurus*.

4. What did *Stegosaurus* have along its back?

a. Long bony plates.
b. Long green stripes.
c. Long black hair.

5. The smallest dinosaurs were the size of . . .

a. snails.
b. chickens.
c. dogs.

6. How many teeth did a *Triceratops* have?

a. Up to 3.
b. Up to 100.
c. Up to 800.

7. *Velociraptor* means . . .

a. "speedy thinker."
b. "speedy thief."
c. "speedy eater."

8. What was an *Ankylosaurus's* scariest weapon?

a. A razor sharp claw
b. Poisonous phlegm
c. A giant, club-tail

9. *T rex* had a lifespan of around . . .

a. 5 years.
b. 30 years.
c. 100 years.

10. *Brachiosaurus* used its huge tail to . . .

a. whip its enemies.
b. carry its young.
c. clear pathways.

15

This or That?

Answer the questions by taking your pick from the following "This or That" choices.

1. Who was smartest?

Velociraptor ☐ or *Stegosaurus* ☐

2. Who was heavier?

Brachiosaurus ☐ or *T rex* ☐

3. What were *Triceratops* horns as long as?

Hockey sticks ☐ or matchsticks ☐

4. Who had the most teeth?

Triceratops ☐ or *T rex* ☐

5. Who was the boniest?

Stegosaurus ☐ or *Velociraptor* ☐

6. How did *Allosaurus* walk?

On two legs ☐ or on four legs ☐

7. Who was the longest?

Spinosaurus ☐ or *Deinonychus* ☐

8. What did a *Parasaurolophus* crest act like?

A magnet ☐ or a trumpet ☐

9. What was *Deinonychus* covered in?

Feathers ☐ or fur ☐

10. What type of eater was *Spinosaurus*?

A herbivore ☐ or a carnivore ☐

11. What does "ceratopian" mean?

"Horned face" ☐ or "Horned foot" ☐

12. Who walked the planet first?

T rex ☐ or *Spinosaurus* ☐

Dino Dig Disaster

These dinosaur discoveries are broken into bits! Circle the dinosaur part that doesn't belong!

Stegosaurus

Velociraptor

Tyrannosaurus rex

Spinosaurus

19

Brain-Buster 2 😊😊

The Big-Buster is back!
You know the rules.

Add up your scores as you go along. The last question is worth 1,000 points. But beware! If you get a question wrong, you're out of the quiz and will lose everything!

For 50 points . . .

What do you call a dinosaur who kills other dinosaurs for food?

A. A predator
B. A herbivore
C. A scavenger
D. Sir!

Score _____

For 100 points . . .

How tall did a *Velociraptor* grow?

A. As tall as a house.
B. As tall as a chicken.
C. As tall as a horse.
D. As tall as a large dog.

Score _____

For 200 points . . .

What were *T rex* bones filled with?

A. Water
B. Nothing
C. Slime
D. Gas

Score _____

For **300** points . . .

Parasaurolophus had very long . . .

A. nostrils.
B. toenails.
C. hair.
D. eyelashes.

Score

For **500** points . . .

What was the weather like during the Jurassic period?

A. Wet and mild
B. Hot and stormy
C. Cold and snowy
D. Dark and windy

Score

For **1,000** points . . .

Deinonychus weighed the same as . . .

A. six cows.
B. three cats.
C. two horses.
D. one human.

Score

Total score

Answers

Pages 2-3
Brainy or Bogus

1. Brainy
2. Brainy
3. Bogus
4. Bogus
5. Brainy
6. Brainy
7. Brainy

8. Brainy
9. Bogus
10. Brainy
11. Bogus
12. Bogus
13. Brainy
14. Bogus

Pages 4-5
Splat Attack

1. *Allosaurus*
2. *Triceratops*
3. *T rex*
4. *Brachiosaurus*
5. *Stegosaurus*

Pages 6-7
Brain-Buster

50 pts – B
100 pts – B
200 pts – D
300 pts – D
500 pts – C
1,000 pts – C

Pages 8–11
Clued Up!

Animal 1 – *Stegosaurus*
Animal 2 – *Tyrannosaurus rex*
Animal 3 – *Triceratops*
Animal 4 – *Brachiosaurus*
Animal 5 – *Velociraptor*
Animal 6 – *Ankylosaurus*
Animal 7 – *Spinosaurus*

Page 13
Dino Dinners

T rex was a carnivore, so he would eat:
Sausage Chicken Ham Rabbit Eggs Duck

The hidden word is "scared."

Pages 14–15
Multi-Choice Challenge

1. B
2. A
3. B
4. A
5. B

6. C
7. B
8. C
9. B
10. A

Answers

Pages 16–17
This or That?

1. *Velociraptor*
2. *Brachiosaurus*
3. Hockey sticks
4. *Triceratops*
5. *Stegosaurus*
6. Two legs

7. *Spinosaurus*
8. Trumpet
9. Feathers
10. Carnivore
11. Horned face
12. *Spinosaurus*

Pages 18–19
Dino Dig Disaster

1. 2. 3. 4.

Pages 20–21
Brain-Buster 2

50 pts – A
100 pts – D
200 pts – B

300 pts – A
500 pts – A
1,000 pts – D